D1707129

DISCARD

AFRICAN WRITERS SERIES

Editorial Adviser: Chinua Achebe

69

FIXIONS

AFRICAN WRITERS SERIES

1 Chinua Achebe: *Things Fall Apart*
2 Cyprian Ekwensi: *Burning Grass*
3 Chinua Achebe: *No Longer at Ease*
4 Kenneth Kaunda: *Zambia Shall be Free*
5 Cyprian Ekwensi: *People of the City*
6 Peter Abrahams: *Mine Boy*
7 James Ngugi: *Weep Not Child*
8 John Reed and Clive Wake (Editors): *A Book of African Verse*
9 Richard Rive: *Modern African Prose*
10 Paul Edwards (Editor): *Equiano's Travels*
11 T. M. Aluko: *One Man, One Matchet*
12 William Conton: *The African*
13 Mongo Beti: *Mission to Kala*
14 Richard Rive, Alex La Guma, James Matthews and Alf Wannenburgh: *Quartet*
15 David Cook (Editor): *Origin East Africa*
16 Chinua Achebe: *Arrow of God*
17 James Ngugi: *The River Between*
18 Obotunde Ijimere: *The Imprisonment of Obatala and other plays*
19 Cyprian Ekwensi: *Lokotown and other stories*
20 Mugo Gatheru: *Child of Two Worlds*
21 John Munonye: *The Only Son*
22 Lenrie Peters: *The Second Round*
23 Ulli Beier (Editor): *The Origin of Life and Death*
24 Aubrey Kachingwe: *No Easy Task*
25 Elechi Amadi: *The Concubine*
26 Flora Nwapa: *Efuru*
27 Francis Selormey: *The Narrow Path*
29 Ferdinand Oyono: *Houseboy*
30 T. M. Aluko: *One Man, One Wife*
31 Chinua Achebe: *A Man of the People*
32 T. M. Aluko: *Kinsman and Foreman*
33 Stanlake Samkange: *On Trial for my Country*
34 Cosmo Pieterse (Editor): *Ten One-Act Plays*
35 Alex La Guma: *A Walk in the Night and other stories*
36 James Ngugi: *A Grain of Wheat*
37 Lenrie Peters: *Satellites*

38 Oginga Odinga: *Not yet Uhuru*
39 Ferdinand Oyono: *The Old Man and the Medal*
40 S. A. Konadu: *A Woman in Her Prime*
41 Amu Djoleto: *The Strange Man*
42 Kofi Awoonor: *Poems from Ghana*
43 Ayi Kwei Armah: *The Beautyful Ones Are Not Yet Born*
44 Elechi Amadi: *The Great Ponds*
45 John Munonye: *Obi*
46 Dennis Brutus: *Letters to Martha and other poems*
47 Tayeb Salih: *The Wedding of Zein*
48 Bakare Gbadamosi and Ulli Beier: *Not Even God is Ripe Enough*
49 Kwame Nkrumah: *Neo-Colonialism*
50 J. P. Clark: *America, their America*
51 James Ngugi: *The Black Hermit*
52 Sahle Sellassie: *The Afersata*
53 Peter K. Palangyo: *Dying in the Sun*
54 Robert Serumaga: *Return to the Shadows*
55 S. A. Konadu: *Ordained by the Oracle*
56 Flora Nwapa: *Idu*
57 Mbella Sonne Dipoko: *Because of Women*
58 Ulli Beier (Editor): *Political Spider and other Stories*
59 Bediako Asare: *Rebel*
60 Luis Bernardo Honwana: *We Killed Mangy-Dog and other stories*
61 Rems Nna Umeasiegbu: *The Way We Lived*
62 Christopher Okigbo: *Labyrinths*
63 Sembene Ousmane: *God's Bits of Wood*
64 Cosmo Pieterse (Editor): *Seven South African Poets*
65 Duro Ladipo: *Three Plays*
66 Tayeb Salih: *Season of Migration to the North*
67 Nkem Nwanko: *Danda*
68 Gabriel Okara: *The Voice*
69 Taban lo Liyong: *Fixions*
70 T. M. Aluko: *Chief The Honourable Minister*

FIXIONS

& other stories
by Taban lo Liyong

HEINEMANN
LONDON NAIROBI IBADAN

Heinemann Educational Books Ltd
48 Charles Street, London WIX 8AH
PMB 5205 Ibadan · POB 25080 Nairobi

EDINBURGH MELBOURNE TORONTO
AUCKLAND HONG KONG SINGAPORE

SBN 435 90069 2

Set in Monotype Bembo
and printed in Great Britain by
Cox & Wyman Ltd
London, Fakenham and Reading

CONTENTS

	Page
The Old Man of Usumbura and His Misery	1
Sages and Wages	11
Stare Decisis Deo	21
Tombe 'Gworong's Own Story	25
He and Him	31
Lexicographicide	39
A Traveller's Tale	47
Ododo pa Apwoyo Gin ki Lyech	53
Fixions	77

THE OLD MAN
OF USUMBURA
AND HIS MISERY

THERE was an old man of Usumbura who was very rich. This old man of Usumbura. He was so rich he had eight thousand cows. This rich old man of Usumbura. With these cows he married for himself sixty-five wives. The old man of Usumbura. He was so healthy that he had three hundred children from these wives. Our healthy man of Usumbura. He was so happy and successful that with industry his wealth increased manifoldly. This happy successful and industrious man of Usumbura. He and all the members of his family were so lucky none of them ever felt sick. These lucky people of Usumbura. All his life he had never known the pangs of sorrow or grief. This lucky Usumburan.

There was another old man of Kigali who was very poor. This old man of Kigali. He was thoroughly sunk in misery. This miserable man of Kigali. His eyes were always red with weeping. The eyes of the man of Kigali. He was rich once. This previously rich man of Kigali. But he had lost all his worldly goods to the last bit. This erstwhile rich man of Kigali. He had not even a wife left him

now. This old man of Kigali. Not even a child was
left to console him in his old age and poverty. This
bereft man of Kigali. All day long he mourned for
his lost cows. This old man of Kigali. He also wept
for his dead wives. This single man of Kigali. He
wept all night for his dead children. This mourning
old man of Kigali. He always cried, 'Oh, my
misery! Oh, my misery!' This miserable old
man.

The rich, happy old man of Usumbura and the
poor, miserable old man of Kigali were friends.
These old men of Usumbura and Kigali.

One day the rich old man of Usumbura went on
a journey. This rich old man of Usumbura. He
went to Kigali. This rich man of Usumbura. He
went to visit his poor friend. This rich man of
Usumbura. When he arrived at Kigali he was
struck by his friend's cry of 'Oh, my misery' and
became sympathetic. This happy man of Usumbura. He asked to be shown the nature of misery.
This healthy man of Usumbura. The miserable
man of Kigali tried to discourage him. This
adventurous old man of Usumbura. But he would
hear none of that. This happy healthy rich old man
of Usumbura. He seemed to have been so bored
with his constantly happy life that he needed a
change. This lucky man of Usumbura. Any kind
of a change would be better than that drab
happy life. That life of this unmiserable man of

3

The Old Man of Usumbura and His Misery

Usumbura. At last the miserable old man of Kigali consented to give a slice of misery to his happy friend from Usumbura. These old friends of Kigali and Usumbura.

They appointed a date when misery would be conveyed from Kigali to Usumbura. These old men of Kigali and Usumbura. The rich man's sons were to come and convey misery from Kigali to Usumbura. These lucky sons of Usumbura. They were to transport misery from the poor man's home to their rich father's home. These happy obedient sons of Usumbura.

On the day appointed all the one hundred and fifty-one sons started off early for Kigali. These fat children of Usumbura. They ran part of the way. These expectant sons of Usumbura. Instead of taking two days to reach Kigali they did it in one day. These impatient and obedient sons of Usumbura. It was evening when they reached Kigali. These heirs of Usumbura. They rested a while but ate nothing in Kigali. These worthy agents of fate. In the evening they insisted they be given misery straightaway to take home to Usumbura. These playful sons of Usumbura. The old man of Kigali suggested they wait till the following morning. This unknown old man of Kigali. But as would be expected these hot-headed sons of Usumbura would not like a delay. These children full of great expectations. The old man of Kigali thought the

1

time had come to give them misery. And he was right, this old man of Kigali.

The old man of Kigali gave them a very large straw bundle. This large straw bundle. This bundle was tightly tied with ropes. The tightly-tied bundle. It contained the very misery so greatly desired by the old rich Usumbura man. This loved misery. It contained the misery so desired by the hundred and fifty-one children. This loved misery.

The old man of Kigali gave the sons of Usumbura a few orders. This knowing man of Kigali. The children were never to tamper with the luggage. They were to carry it right before their father. These inquisitive children. The children shouted for joy. These live children of Usumbura. They managed in their own way to convey this heavy burden a few steps at a time. Nothing was heavier to each of them than this pregnant egg. The incurious Usumburans.

When the bundle had left Kigali the old man started to smile. This prescient man of Kigali.

Midway between Kigali and Usumbura these boys stopped. These obedient children of Usumbura. Some of them said they were tired. These lively children of Usumbura. Others thought they needed to enjoy a bit of the sunset. These observant children of Usumbura. A few thought a little rest was in order. These restless children of Usumbura. One admitted he really needed a relaxation. These playful children of Usumbura. One said the rope looked green. These children who can see green at night. One thought the rope had surely loosened since they had left Kigali. One wagered he would loosen one, just one of the knots. These indefatigable children of Usumbura. One said he was tickled by misery on the side next to him. These sensible children of Usumbura. One boy exhibited with triumph a rope unloosened. These active children of Usumbura. The elder ordered there be no tampering with misery. This orderly elder son. But another thought only blind people carry what they cannot see. These seeing children of Usumbura. So an argument grew up between the children who wanted to see misery before it reached their father and those who wanted their father to see misery first. These factious children. While the argument was in progress some children stayed unconcerned. These apathetic and reflective children. But a few boys were busy with their nimble hands. These constant active few.

The bundle became smaller and smaller as the argument became louder and louder. This bundle and strife. Nothing substantial could be seen yet from the bundle although brother was already abusing brother. This cause of strife. Blows started to rain on brothers' heads. These headbreaking blows. At last a handful of the luggage remained. That fatal unknown. Curiosity brought brothers together to see this famed thing. The curiosity that killed the cat. They squeezed together, they held their breaths, they were ready to see, they were all attention. These humans.

When the bundle was opened, nothing was seen. The cheated sights. Only a little whirring sound was heard. The noise that has no path. It sounded like a mosquito. This child of the egg.

Now that there was no more misery to carry home, what were these boys to carry home to their father? These obedient boys of Usumbura. One brother's hands were already striking another for having opened the bundle. These useful hands we have. Another hit another on the head, another smote another, another slew another, another clubbed another, another speared another, another strangled another, another castrated another, another drank another's blood. These killers of their own brothers. Now only fifty brothers remained in the internecine war. These brother-killing brothers. Three minutes later we see only three blood-intoxicated brothers. These committed brothers. Two brothers have ganged up on a brother. The unhappy company. The last round ends with brother killing brother. Oh, the fatal end. Death, you have reaped a rich harvest. Death that levels all. Alas, who will inform the rich man of Usumbura? That rich, happy, wealthy, un-miserable old man of Usumbura.

But one boy remained alive. This unlucky boy of Usumbura. He had always been a coward. This life-preserving son of his mother. He had hidden away during the life-destroying brotherly exercises. That fatal exercise. He became the messenger of misery to his father. Oh, the fatal messenger that should never arrive. Out of breath with sorrow and running, he approached his expectant father with the news. This sorrow-filled son of his beaming father. The father anticipated an advance information on the approaching misery. This happy father of Usumbura. He asked how near misery was. This impatient father of Usumbura. He repeated the question with anger. This father who can't even wait for his son to regain his breath. He struck the son once for the delay. This father who had never known how to strike a blow. But only good news comes out pat. This bad news which demands a cautious framing. The son started to sob, more from internal blows. This vessel of deaths. At last he said misery had escaped. The misery that travels in the air. The old man of Usumbura was so mad he struck his son dead instantly. This happy, rich, healthy, misery-less old father of Usumbura.

The rich, happy, healthy, worry-less old man of Usumbura has now killed his son. This father who does not know misery. The wife whose son was struck dead started to mourn. In this home that has never known mourning. Other wives realized that she had deserved such a treatment for a long time past. Oh, human wisdom that always condemns those who are afflicted. This mother's wrong deeds consist of insolence. Oh, the home that never knew insolence. And her son was said to have been disrespectful to their worthy husband. Oh, the love that is intensified by the degradation of others. He was the only black sheep in this snow-white home. Give a dog a name and you hang him. His mother left the home of the rich old man that very night. The darkest of nights. She did not carry her son's corpse with her. The lifeless luggage. It was her share of misery she took along with her. Oh, misery that curiosity brings.

The old man of Usumbura set out that very night to find his other hundred and forty-nine sons. These all-virtuous sons. He took along with him his fifty-five wives. The wives that love their husband and never do wrong. Husband and wives went to find sons and misery. Oh, obsessions that are so dear to the hearts.

On the way the smell of new blood tickled their noses. Smell that travels in the wind. They became wild. These good people. Soon they stepped on cadaver instead of earth. Oh, organic flesh and earth. They kissed their lifeless sons because there was nothing else to do. These virtuous sons and wives. They had no more stomach for misery. These misery-filled parents.

They abandoned their happy husband to his fate and went off to their several parents' homes. These good wives of Usumbura. They took with them all their daughters and shares of wealth. These unlike-the-other-wife wives.

At last the old man was left to bear his misery alone. The old man who had wanted so much to see misery. He sang a song called 'Oh, my misery! Oh, my misery!' This rich, healthy, happy, misery-less old man of Usumbura.

SAGES
AND WAGES

We hold these as truths, self-evident:
A reader must not yawn
During the yarn
Without the loss (of his head)
Or that, of the writer's.
The Lay of the Ancient Optics Grinder

THIS is how she was born:

There was no midwife or nurse or any special helper whatsoever around. Her mother tried to help her deliver, but had difficulties holding her to one spot. For it must be remembered that this was her second baby, and the delivery of the first had required the attendance of five of our athletic women. For some reason invisible to all, she would break loose, and dash one hundred metres, and would have run more, had she not been overtaken and pinned down. She would cry: 'Mama, choke me! Choke me,' and her mother would be at it till the eyes of both mother and daughter were red. But she was stronger than her mother, and the latter ended up by relaxing her grip before the daughter was weakened enough or had the satisfaction from the choking. As I was saying, that was during her first delivery. Our story, however, concerns the second delivery.

Her mother, finding that she was alone (all of the athletic girls had gone off somewhere to practise) did the best she could, viz., bound her on a pillar so that her hands and legs met on the other side of the pillar and a large bandage or sash bound her mid-region firmly on to the pillar. This ingenuity served the double purpose of holding her to a spot and, whenever she cried: 'Mama, throttle me' her mother simply responded by tightening the sash. (Her trouble was *not* in her throat. I'll tell you where it was, if you really want to know.)

Needless to say, in due course her tummy was flattened. To untie her from the pillar with minimum loss of time and life was the problem her mother had not foreseen. It took time. And even when it was accomplished, to get her out of the sitting position (a dangerous sitting position as she was sitting on her new-born baby) proved a difficulty for anile wit. Grandma simply pushed her backwards, dislocating in the process, the child's neck so that later she moved with her head at a tilt like a bent wind-vane whose north pointed downward rather than northward, and whose south arm was an arrested arrow aimed at the stars. That was not the only damage. Her head was indented like a

clay egg – a flatness was introduced into the figure.
This last occurrence was stranger still: instead of
crying when it recovered from the shock, as other
babies do, it laughed. And to laugh it continued,
throughout its living days.

'As I always do, at this time of the day, which is
most appropriate for the task at hand, and therefore
never to be missed, as the rewards are many, and
anybody in possession of her mind has to be careful
of such things at this regular time or at other times
when to do this would also do, in fact should be a
must, as such a well-given chance needs not be
missed because missed it may never be admitted
again or would appear like saying: "it happened
yesterday exactly at this very time" when times are
never the same; as I feel that I must really do it
without fail as I have really done all these years the
way I am doing now and have never missed the
chance, the time, the opportune moment, I am
therefore glad that I have done it because there was
no objection; what is that noise? Yes, I am infinitely
grateful that I am able to do exactly this thing
which I am doing; that javelin I threw this morning
fell just four inches beyond the point I threw yesterday, it is therefore a fair calculation that tomorrow, everything being equal, I should be in a

position to throw just one-half inch beyond this point and the day after another one-half of one-half inch will bring me to the same distance as our captain. As I keep on doing this every hour, except when occasions necessitate, I am grateful that I am not denied doing it. My knees still are able to rest on the board and I am ready to benefit from this; if the day after tomorrow comes (it is bound to, everything being equal), me and the captain/the captain and I?/who will be captain (the longest thrower is captain). I am always grateful there are aids to the performance of the *vita*; (*vita* – Latin, life: *Ars longa vita est longa, longa? kurt?*). Since I was young, seeing this done and being told to do it (didn't find it bad at all) and the doing of it being vital; (*ars longa vita brevis est*). I know it that three hours have already passed while I dedicated myself to this duty; three miles I can now run in exactly one minute, but I am still seventeen years old compared to the captain who accomplished the same distance in fifty-four seconds when her age is already forty, T t tra, l ab ba cir stan cum ces phy graph hmn l you she that this in on at aton afin onat thishe. The greatest pleasure that always comes to me is in seeing that no objection is raised against my this daily request though I sometimes do it at necessary times for example that day last week when I claimed the captain's far distance for mine and the knowledge you withheld from their eyes; I always

dream, I wonder why, that each moment my spear
hit ground *that* noise disappeared. All in all, always
at this time, or when occasions arise, I shall promptly do just this for its vital importance; food should
be ready now, I wish my sister does not laugh *so*.'

She died amid laughter (from her sister). Even
while the doctor was passing judgement about her
death, the laughter continued as ever, quite oblivious of the fact that conditions had changed, at
least for others. One strange thing happened,
though, which supplies the first footnote to the
occasion. Their mother, contrary to all practices,
refused to believe that her daughter was dead. This
could not be tolerated. If all mothers followed suit
there wouldn't be any more respect for our doctors.
Promptly, therefore the police were telephoned
and within no time, they arrived in their ayrecop-
ter, arrested her as they would a traitor, and
whisked her off. This action pleased the village's
poor, as they were sure there was one mouth less
for the feast which follows the doctors' certification.

Our neighbour, and one neighbour alone, would
have posed a problem for the officers of the law.
But she was still in the athletic field while this
arrest was being made. The arrested mother had
told her a story. It was this:

On two separate occasions, seventeen and fifteen years ago, she (the arrested mother) had ventured beyond the permitted limit of our country. Each time she returned just in time to cry: 'Mama, choke me!' What happened behind those mountains (let me add that our land is actually an island bounded by a circle of a mountain) was her participation in an athletic contest in broad jump across a pond. It was a daily exercise and the athletes were encouraged to do it as long as they are not tired, tiredness being defined as being unable to cross the pond thrice; of course if you don't jump clear, you fall into the water and had the nasty experience of being pricked by flowering water lilies.

That was just a by-the-way. The point is this: the mother (arrested) claimed her children could not die. Now if our witness had said that the dead daughter was not dead, the doctor would have found himself in trouble: where would he get another weapon to counteract this? As it is, the doctor was lucky, but we are cheated of a spectacular incident in the operation of our laws.

For our consolation, we have this: Just as the feasting was continuing, in fact at its merriest, there appeared out of nowhere, a man in this women world. The drummers' hands stopped in mid-air:

their eyes were on this new phenomenon; the dancers panted as a fleeing culprit would when overtaken in his flight: the speed of stopping was tremendous; the singers would have even re-captured the echoes before they were fully realized; in fact the stoppage was total, that is, if we ignore the laughter.

'Why all this mourning?' the illustrious one asked. Nobody had the voice to speak, but one hand (followed by another) rose by degrees and finally its finger transfixed (through the space) the corpse in the middle of the court. There was an universal anxiety: expecting the unknown is so bewitching!

'Why mourn ye?' he asked.

'Lord, you know as well as we do that our sister is dead,' a voice had the courage born of total belief (in the doctor) to inform the illustrious one.

He, on his own accord, taking off his tunic and waving it about like a wand, and exposing his sides to everybody around said: 'She is not dead' but had the misfortune of being interrupted by doubt-ing: 'Oh! Oh! Oh!' from all around. But he was not the person to be silenced by doubters. With flaming eyes he proceeded very casually to finish his sentence (but of course he had to begin from the beginning – just like himself): 'She is not dead,' he said, 'but asleep!'

But 'asleep' was a new word to these women. We

must remember that they are athletes, now athletes do not 'sleep': they are forever athletizing: awake or dreaming.

'Prove it, prove it!' were the demands from all around. There was no sense in learning the word 'asleep', since it did not feature in the Athletic Records, it was possibly a meteoric word. (However, the Master of Ceremonies had the presence of mind to record it down for conveyance to the museum after this hullabaloo was over.) But 'prove it' had a legal validity since it was the most athletic challenge synonymous with: 'Make thy vauntings true.'

He, of the lightning eyes, divining their doubt and challenge went coolly about it, like the practised magician.

'I will show you. But, follow my directions,' he said. At that, these women were all alert; the drunkards all of a sudden sobered, you could see that one word then possessed the centre of the floor in their minds: the athletic word: 'Ready.'

He nodded, in appreciation. 'Bring a black goat here!' Done. 'With this sharp sword, cut it at one blow right through the middle from head to tail!' The captain in cutology did it.

'Choose two runners!' The captain and her second assistant (the real assistant was dead, you are of course aware) volunteered. 'You take this at your best speed to that tree over yonder, you see that fig tree' (he indicated the one towards the East), 'take this part, hang it at an arm's reach from the ground.' Second assistant disappeared. 'You, take this to that other fig tree,' pointing to the one furthest west. The captain went and returned at the same time (time: ·05 seconds) with her second assistant.

'Now, follow this very carefully,' he said, dazzling them with his flashing eyes, 'get on your knees. Done? Close your eyes. Done? Seal them with your hands. Done? Keep silent. Remain so till I tell you to talk and open your eyes again!'

Complete darkness and silence ensued, that is if we disregard that knowing laughter.

STARE
DECISIS
DEO

This story was first published under the title 'Parable from Another Land' in *Motive*, Nashville, Tennessee in March 1966.

Accept him.
As he is.
So sang the Dove.

MONKEY heard that while going to visit Python that Christmas day. When he arrived, Python called aloud to his mother like this:

'Mummy, Mummy, bring some food. My friend Monkey has arrived.'

Monkey was tired and hungry. 'I am so lucky,' he thought, 'I will eat to death.' He rushed to the floor where the well-cooked meal was placed.

'Monkey,' said Python, 'go and wash your hands. Nobody eats with dirty hands.'

He went, washed his hands, and hurried to where the food was.

'Do you call those hands washed?' was what Python said, 'Have some sense. Those hands are black and dirty. Use soap and warm water.'

Monkey went and did so. He returned with clean hands, palm out.

'Now, Monkey, where were you raised? How can you come to table so dirty, so smelly, so black? Get that blackness off your hands.'

Monkey took a butcher's knife, skinned away the black skin on his palms. The palms turned red, red with blood. Tears dropped from his eyes as blood dropped from his hands.

He was still hungry. He came to eat.

'How can you be so uncultured? So unintelligent? Don't touch my food with your blood. I am no cannibal.' Those were Python's words.

Monkey started for home.

The Dove was singing:

Accept him,
As he is.

Another Christmas day came. Python was going to visit Monkey.

Accept him,
As he is.
Accept him,
As he is.

He heard the Dove sing.

'Countryman,' said Monkey to Python, 'you are most welcome.' Python spread his twenty-foot length on the floor, filling almost every space.

'Mama Monkey,' her son called, 'bring us the feast.' Food was brought and placed on the floor. Monkey sat on his haunches, and laid his hands on his knees.

'Now Python, my countryman,' said Monkey, 'get seated.'

Python coiled himself into a heap like tyres of different sizes.

'Mistah, we don't call that "sittin'",' said Monkey. 'Now, get seated like other folks. See what I mean?'

Python uncoiled himself. He pushed the greater part of his twenty feet outside the hut. His head was near the pot of food.

'I didn't tell you to lie on your belly. You must learn to sit, and to sit properly inside a house.' Monkey said like that.

Python assembled all of himself inside the hut. He started to sit, on his tail. His head went up, up, up, till it pierced through the roof.

Monkey ate the food. He took a cutlass and chopped off seven feet from Python's tail. Python jerked up the bulk of his squirting length through the grass roof.

They both heard the Dove singing:

> *Accept him,*
> *As he is.*
> *Accept him,*
> *As he is.*

Everyday the Dove sings:

> *Accept them, as they are.*
> *Accept them, as they are.*
> *as they are.*
> *as they are.*

TOMBE
'GWORONG'S
OWN STORY

To understand this story there are three things you must know. One is that I am a Tombe 'Gworong – that is, of the tribe that eats people. We are not cannibals, though. For cannibalism means a human being, in his human condition, eating another human being either as food or physic or both. Ours is not that. When our people want to eat people they become leopards first, and then, as leopards, they seize a man, or a woman, or a child, and even other animals such as goats, cows, buffaloes, or birds like chicken and vultures, and eat them. I do not know how we change from human to leopard shape. But it is a kind of metamorphosis we have been able to achieve, and are known for by all the tribes around us. These adjoining tribes know it too well, in fact. For, you see, when another tribesman has taken our cattle, or taken away a wife from one of us, we meet and go to see what we can do. This being, in most cases, all of our people – men, women, and children – becoming leopards, and also inviting squirrels and knives and anything we can convert into leopards (most earthly things actually do, for example knives, arrows, stones, and cats, have been known to yield) and with this large number of leopards we make the greatest amount of noise in and around the home of those who took from us. Not only that: we also put herbs into their wells so that they get diarrhoea and come out at night to help themselves, so that we, the leopards, jump on them, stick our fingers into their flesh, and our sharp teeth into their flesh, drag them away amid noise and eat as many of them as we can. We also eat the cows. After we have done enough of that, we reclaim our human shapes.

I have been told that we are required to throw up any human flesh we have eaten. Also that one of us, who had poor teeth, lost some of them on an old woman – her skin was so tough it pulled out the tooth of the man-turned-leopard. When he became man again, of course he lacked a tooth. Those of us who want to go in style, become leopards while still wearing their shirts. And in the evenings when going to the people who took from us (who, I am told, sit in their compound, warming themselves by the fire around which they sit, and by this time would have their backs turned to the fire and would be holding spears, on the look out for us) may wait for awhile till these people are going to their various huts and then jump on one of them and carry him off. Although the man being carried off may make noise on account of the

fingers and teeth of the leopard, his friends do not
spear – they do not know of the two animals which
is the leopard and which is their man. Also, some of
these people not wanting to come out of their huts
at night to pee because they think we are nearby,
sometimes use a bamboo pipe jutting from their
huts for peeing. One of us caught them doing this
and hit the bamboo right inside. There was noise.
At one time when I was eating chickens (turned
leopard, of course) a lame man spoke aloud from
one of the huts that the white cock in the cot was
for paying his medicine man. I left it, took all the
rest, tore out their intestines, and emptied them
into the well where they get their drinking water. I
must also mention the fact that my aunt gave birth
to a baby. When he was a day old, at night he
became a cat and was chasing away rats up on the
roof of our hut. My aunt touched the cat with the
stick our women use for making bread and had her
baby back again.

The next thing you must know in order to
understand this story is this. One day there was a
race for all animals of the bush. Then, the fastest and
subtlest animal was the hare. So when all the
animals were ready, the lion gave the signal for go.
And everything which can run, crawl, slide, or fly,
was at it. Hare, reaching the end of the race, pre-
pared to sit down on the marking post in order to
see who would be next. When he was about to sit

down, he heard a voice behind him: 'Don't sit on me. I am already there.' It was chameleon. (When the race was about to start he had clung to Hare's tail.)

The third thing you have to know is this. A certain chief's daughter once thought everybody did not suit her aesthetic taste. Some of the chief's sons who wanted her for a wife had a head too large, or teeth very long, legs made like bows, were too tall or too short, did not laugh musically, and so on. When all the men who wanted her left her alone, a man came, who fulfilled all her prescription of what her man should be. She went with him to his home. At night when they were about to sleep, he took off his clothes. She looked at him and found he was a different person. He looked as ordinary as one of those men she had sent away. So she got out a knife and cut him to pieces. When she was going to throw the cut pieces away, the man part of the dead man jumped about dancing and singing a song, nodding his head. It finally jumped and disappeared right into her woman part.

Here now is the story. When we are still men, we do not expose our heads to be knocked off or pierced through. We do not live when that is done. When we are changed into leopards, we mind about our backs, especially where our tails begin. When we are leopards, our human heads are where our leopard backs are.

HE
AND HIM

For Onen and Tom

A STORY doesn't have to have many characters in it. In this one, for example, we have two people, and we feel they are enough. One is he, the visitor from the country, and the other is him, the object of the visit. The subject, I may add, is the visit of he to town.

As we feel that what he ate for breakfast that morning has no relevance whatsoever on the visit, nor the colour of the sky while he passed through the countryside, nor how sharp his nose is, nor how blue his eyes – in fact, since we feel that these extraneous things other writers use for fleshing up scanty stories are not constitutional ingredients of the story, we shall cut them out – for the readers' benefit. We understand our readers are busy people, rushing from one phase of life to another.

One thing we must say, though: he coughed. That is important. Another: his friend smoked. Yet another: they both loved reading; this is something they picked up in their youth when they were in school together.

He had been in the country for some years now. Exactly how many does not affect the substance of the story very much. What absolutely matters is that whereas things stood still in the country, except the growth of weeds more than that of crops, and the multiplication of pigs in excess of cows, in the city changes had already become so topical that he had decided to come and see for himself.

Upon reaching his friend's house, and finding that nobody answered to his knocks or calls – or answered them as quickly as he had the patience to wait for – quite a long patience, as you understand, he was a simple farmer from the countryside – he pushed the door open, went in, and chose a chair which looked comfortable enough for a farmer (please don't think that farmers do not like to sit down on a soft, comfortable chair), held his hat on his hand, lifted one of his heavy shoed legs and placed it on top of the other and settled down to a profound absorption of the room's content with his eyes. Presently he looked like an ancient statue. Just at that moment his friend comes in from the other end of the house, pulls him up, and pushes him out. He nearly fell; if he had fallen and injured himself, that would have been very bad. Farmers have to be healthy so that they can take care of their plants and livestock. No weed stops growing during a farmer's sickness. Then his friend stopped, passed his hands over his face. In the next moment, with a broad smile, extended his right hand to his friend for a brisk, warm handshake. The townman's explanation came with a chill: 'You are welcome into my house.'

'But wait out there a moment,' he was running into the house, from which he presently emerged with a pair of sandals, exactly like those on his feet, and ordered his guest to put them on. The farmer's boots were shoved into a chute which yawned nearby. The two friends went in, and he was led to sit down on one of the two chairs in the centre of the room. Embarrassed, he twisted his hat in his hand. The friend noticed this and relieved him of it, took it and deposited it in another chute (resembling the one for shoes outside), came back and sat down. 'How are you, my dear?' he said, without passion or emotion. (You understand, our man from the countryside is used to warmth in personal contact – nay, he even still has feelings for the beautiful, dirty, gruntling, snub-nosed piglets, and he caresses hay.)

He answered: 'I am fine, although I cough –' but before he had amended it by 'I cough a little,' his friend had shot up like a bullet and ordered him to stand up as well. He was marched into another room. 'In case your cough might come upon you,

you must understand that you can cough freely here.'

As he had not yet seen that morning's town paper, he wondered if his friend could get it for him. 'Yes,' and 'stand up,' and 'let's go.' His friend marched ahead like a wooden soldier. He followed him from behind. This promises to be a memorable day, was the thought taking shape slowly in his mind. 'This is our reading room. You may feel free to read everything in this room, except nothing.' After that the town paper was thrust into his hands, while his friend disengaged the daily reading record from the wall, and brought it to him to sign and record the titles of the works, their authors, the substances, and his critical commentaries about them. 'This is very important. Absolutely,' was the accompanying order.

After a while, obviously he had been jostled too much, measured in a farmer's way, too much for two complete days' work – he began to yawn. But just when his jaws were widely distended, with a 'whop!' he found the expansion of his mouth arrested. His friend's left hand blocked the mouth to make sure the yawning was not consummated, and with the other hand the farmer was being pulled (actually dragging him) to an adjacent cubicle. 'Yawn away all you like here, as freely as you like. In the future if you feel it coming, make a dash for this place. These amenities are here to be used, and must be used, otherwise how can we justify their existence?'

It was now mealtime. Two saucers of salt were brought to them in the sitting-room. 'Eat. This is the first course.' His host proceeded to lick away the salt with the greatest appetite. He did, likewise. Then they went to the salad room. Here was the instruction: 'With the salad, it is different. You eat the salad *first* and the dressing later.' They set to like pigs.

Midway through salad, he felt uncomfortable. 'I – I – I –' he faltered.

'You, you, you – you what? Say it quickly. Quick, lest you do the wrong thing in this place.'

'It is coming, oh, I feel it, it . . .' his eyes were blinking, he was tense all over.

'What?' was the order.

'Cough' the answer.

'Then run to the first room to your left – the coughing room.'

When he returned, he followed his friend through various courses up to the place where you pick up your meat in one corner of the house, go and chew it in the next (going anti-clockwise) go and swallow it in the third, and rinse away the taste of *that* particular taste of meat in the fourth with a glass of water. Needless to add that the meat was not salted (because they had already eaten, or deposited, their salt in their stomachs in the sitting-room); and needless also to add that the meat was not cooked.

As soon as the meal was over, they went inevitably to the room which had a roaring fire, many cigarettes and hangers for coats and shirts. His host told him to follow exactly what he was going to do. Upon saying that, he removed his coat and placed it on a hanger. The farmer did the same. 'Take off that thing, too,' pointing to the farmer's vest (he himself did not wear one). 'You may cast it into the fire. When you feel sticky, rush to the bathroom.' The host then took a cigarette, lit it, and chose one of those chairs nearest the hot fire. His friend did likewise. For some time then, they went on doing things in this fashion: inhaling cigarettes to smoke their meat, and exposing their stomachs as near as possible to the fire so that its heat may cook the meat they had eaten raw.

This process was interrupted from time to time, however, by one of these gentlemen rushing to the coughing room. Nine minutes, however, was the time allotted for this. Then the host got up as if pricked by a child's pin and said in a stern voice: 'Follow, quick. I have thought of something.' They rushed through two doors naked. At the end of the running, the host started laughing earnestly and boisterously. (It was a genuine laughter – *his eyes watered*!) He had remembered an old joke which was a very 'suxessful relaxant'.

He and Him

Before the farmer left, however, he was ushered into the instruction room and taught the importance of doing things rightly in their assigned places. 'That is absolutely important. Absolutely.'

LEXICO-
GRAPHICIDE

For Amos Tutuola from whom I have learnt many important things, the greatest being that the most important virtue is courage.

T HE following six notes were found by the bed of the victim (found dead). Here is his biographical background: At the age of seven he left school on the ground that being in school was a waste of time. In the next three months he wrote articles which appeared even in *The Light* and drew a lot of deserved praise. You need not be reminded that *The Light* is our equivalent of *The Times*. For some unknown reason, he abandoned writing and was never heard from for quite a while. The next piece of information comes from me. I got it because I used to go to visit him. He said that he had written plenty of short stories, on the average of four in a day. Why weren't they published? Editors wouldn't dare print them. When I failed even to have a look at them, I turned to cursing our editors who are so sales-conscious and government-control conscious that they would never print an extraordinary, or extraordinarily written, story.

But he was busy, he said. He planned to become the ruler of our island – a total dictator of it. Once a dictator, he would personally supervise the writing of our Zed dictionary. Zed is the only language of our island. It is spoken by practically all the island's 125,000 people. It has about 50,000 words. Communication between our people and yours are very, very infrequent, for no commercial and other interests pull foreigners to our island. And we are so proud, the last thing an islander would do is to go out. In fact, even without a dictator, the island was almost already sealed off from the outside world. While in office, he would make it complete: the sealing off, I mean. Now about the dictionary, before I forget. It was (he used the word *is*, while telling me) to be different from all others on these grounds: it was going to be the only dictionary for our island; everybody was to be issued with a copy at the beginning of our year – in May, that is; everybody was to use only words (even grunts) printed in the dictionary or else face death. It was easy to find out defaulters. Every Saturday our people go to the market to receive their weekly rations of food. The market has instruments which read minds, and can detect the presence of a new word, a different idea in anybody's head. At the end of each year, that year's edition of the dictionary was to be returned by everybody to the government and exchanged for the current one. But every year, five hundred words were withdrawn from the dictionary.

NOTE I

11 p.m. Been to the sports house today. Saw fighters: boxers. Didn't like it.

4 a.m. Had a bad dream. Dreamt was a boxer. The ordeal! First, you drive to the sports house. Second, you get in. Third, you go to the dressing room. (Wonder why called *dressing* room, when you actually *un*dress there.) However those are some of the inconveniences of living in this obsolescent regime.

NOTE II

10 p.m. Was at the beach today – bathing. Lots of women and men too, exposing their bare flesh to the water, sun and air! Sizes varied; shortness and height. Frankly, all those people may never be able to reclaim their bodies if lost and found!

NOTE III

3 a.m. Feeling tired after writing my theory – nay, gospel – went out for a walk. Slid into a room. Many people there. Music. A lady came on stage – I had thought we have no 'lady' left. But here was one right on the stage. And with an umbrella, too.

Walked about gracefully. Music. Drops umbrella – walks – drops hat – walks, music – take off gloves. I wondered what. But she continued doing what she was doing. Quite oblivious of my questioning looks. Even the dress was now coming off. Her hair reached her back; when bobbed forward, they just covered the breasts, but the breasts had brassieres, and therefore, did not need concealment by the hair. Had underwear. Danced. Frantic. (Narration to be continued.)

NOTE IV

3.30 a.m. Fell asleep. Cannot continue narration above coherently and chronologically. Can remember this very well: was evicted from above house at 4.30 a.m. prompt.

NOTE V

4.30 a.m. Being evicted, walking home, halfway through the journey, accosted by four masked men. Said they have no clothes, no money, no writing things, and had never experienced the joy of dispossessing a man for two whole days. If I pleased, I might oblige them with my coat and its pockets, my eyeglasses and the handles (and case too, if I had any), my watch, its winder, and straps, my shoes and the strings as well, my socks (the holes and smell too are good for them), my trousers (buttons and buttonholes included), the zip too was worth their trouble, if I had a belt, that was also one of their specialties, my shirt, tie, tie-pin, my vest, and my underwear. I did not understand their language.

NOTE VI

5 a.m. Had a long dream tonight. Dreamt was in a classroom – professor (my ambition in childhood). Right there before my pupils, had a most singular intrusion from vandals. A horde of them had the guts to come to *my* classroom, and call me a debtor, to my face! Within no second they had reclaimed every thread I owed them; every one I owed them; every synthetic unit I owed them; every piece of wood or grass they claimed I had taken from them. Then they proceeded to gnaw away at my skin, cubic millimetre by cubic millimetre, beginning from toes and fingers. I felt the reduction coming inevitably, but surely. Fortunately, it was quick – they were numerous. They made a special point to stop before attacking my heart. They even had the common sense to draw the attention of my bewildered students to my heart and saying that this organ 'could have saved me, *but* . . .' The class jeered before that fateful sentence was completed. Then they set to work again, with renewed vigour, with claws and teeth, and enlarged swallowing throats. They spent more time there. It was then an easy matter passing from

lungs and liver to throat and neck. When they reached my head, they had instructions to the owners of my bushy hair to reclaim their things and go. That done, those who wanted my eyelashes, eyebrows, whiskers, moustache, beard (I am an intellectual intelligentsia-convertible, you should know) and any other hair on my face was taken. The skin was removed (together with the ears and the nose), the lower jaws were disengaged, with tongue, teeth, and palates. Two creatures (I think man and wife) sucked my eyeballs at a go. Now the skull was eaten away, and earthworms given the privilege to gobble my brain.

Epilogue: I have remembered a man who used to dodge paying taxes by behaving as if he was mad. He would sing a song, and proceed to drum, and to dance and finally end by watching himself sing-drum-and-dance.

A TRAVELLER'S TALE

THESE are the ingredients: an Italo-American woman, a Negro bum, and an African student. The woman had her regrets and wishes; the Negro his anxiety and insecurity; the African student his readings and hope.

The Italian woman is a housewife and a mother of four: two girls and two boys. Her eldest child is a girl age nineteen and the other children come in somewhere between her age and twelve. She is married to a German but has never had a complete and satisfactory sex-act throughout her twenty years of marriage. She had looked forward to a complete fulfilment in marriage and reasoned that chastity was not too high a price to pay. (She had a puritanical Catholic background. I don't know where she grew up.) But here she was, stuck with a husband who comes to bed like a hunter with gun loaded, aim well taken, and the only business he had in bed was the dropping of the bullet: tup.

She was just getting aroused.

(If she had been more intelligent, she would have tried various do-it-yourself projects, or flashed a lascivious look at a neighbour, or asked a sister in her place of work to help.)

After what is to happen to her in this story, she began to suspect that maybe some of them had been making passes at her but she had been too pre-occupied with herself to have taken notice. (Oddly enough though, she had imagined that her sal-vation would come to her by way of a rape. A rape is at once savage and satisfactory ... if the woman relents in time and becomes accommo-dating. It has the exhilarations of a defloration mixed with fear of the unknown, anger because of suddenness, and memorability because of its rarity.) She wanted to be raped. She looked for-ward to it.

The Negro bum, being a bum of course, and a quiet bum at that, has his keenness of observation, incommunicable desires (some of them still in an amorphous stage and may remain so to the day of his death), and anxieties. We have already said that he is insecure, for obvious reasons. (If one is dumb, it does not mean that one does not observe or see, nor that one has no desires for those things which the rich get by the dollar, the quick-tongued by talking.) Our bum had an eye for flirtatious women, loose women, and women who are also scandal mongers. We shall see.

The African student has just finished reading Spenser's *Faerie Queene*. He is saturated with

49

gallantry. To rescue a damsel in distress, was his highest ambition. (Perhaps it was a 'lady' he should have sought to help, but since he did not look up the finer distinctions in the dictionary, uncon-sciously = wilfully, he stuck to general categories, so that whatever else 'damsel' might also mean did not interest him as much as the sure knowledge that a damsel is a woman.)

It is 5 a.m. New York City, near Harlem and Columbia University. (Any university worth its name must be *in medias res*.) An overpass subway station.

The Italian woman, handbag in left hand and brown lunch bag in the other, has just arrived at the station, panting. She had to hurry in order to catch the 5.07 train for Queens where she works as a laundry hand. She could not see the reasons why she was warmer than usual, despite the hurry. Could it be that (I think) the atmosphere was satur-ated with demons and magis? In any case, she didn't mind being raped straightaway. The good angel who happened to be just around the corner (he is always there – around the corner, the question is: which corner?) heard her prayers. It was his one will then to give her satisfaction that very morning.

The Negro sees her, senses something in the air. Like a hunting dog. What he had been searching all his life (as it were, his Columbus's arrival in the New World) was here, and now, presented to him in a platter. So, it was: now or never. Although there are six or seven other people on the platform, he does not mind them. He walks to her directly and deliberately like someone going for a pre-arranged rendezvous, he clasps her. She lets her bags drop just as deliberately. They lock chests. He unzips, deliberately. She pulls up her dress to her bosom, coolly. He lowers his underwear; she pulls down her underpants . . . and then, o, o, something happened: she blundered. She looked around and saw a volley of eyes. She screamed.

That breaks the spell. The African student rushes in. The Negro abandons her in midair with the kiss he was about to plant on her cheek left forever floating in the air. He is trotting down the stairs. The African student has just caught her and they both dropped down on the platform, she on his lap. She then gives him her most passionate kiss, ecstatic, hot, almost sucking all life out of him. He was almost withered. They remained gripped in embrace for perhaps two minutes, perhaps more, depending on whoever is estimating the time. To him who approved, the time was short; to him who disapproved, it was long; if the participants enjoyed it, the minutes were flying too fast; if they had no more energy, it was tedious.

She now partially recovers and mumbles to herself: why did he want to rape me?, me a mother of four?, and among all these people?

ODODO
PA APWOYO
GIN KI LYECH

*The story of Master Hare
and his friend Jumbe Elephant*

Long, long ago, when the world was very young, there lived two great friends. Their names were Master Hare and Jumbe Elephant. Their friendship was so strong they would even share the smallest eatable ant. They lived with their mothers in the jungle, where the tree trunks were big, very big, bigger than a man's chest.

One year a big famine fell. Everybody was hungry. Jumbe Elephant was so hungry that his long ribs looked like frames for a cage.

Then clouds started to gather in the sky. Cloud was piled on top of cloud. The sky became thick and dark, like the inside of a blanket. It was so thick that the monkey, who is reputed the most cowardly of all the animals in the whole wide jungle, thought the end of the world had come. He preferred to die before the sky fell and crushed everybody on earth to death. So he went, tore off a small piece of creeping plant, and hanged himself.

It only rained, but rained hard, with flood. The next day, the animals started preparing to dig their fields. They wanted to plant food so that there would be no more famine.

Jumbe Elephant's mother was called Min-Jumbe. She was very very old and had grey hair on her head, and all her teeth were not in her mouth. Her skin was wrinkled like a flat bicycle tube. One day, Min-Jumbe called her son to her and patted him on the ears. She then spoke to him like this:

'Jumbe my son, my son, with no father, you see that it is now raining. We must plant food. We want to plant peas, peas, peas. You must eat plenty of peas so that you grow big, big, big, like your father. You must grow big so that when you walk, the lion and the hippo can hear your heavy foot-steps when you are still a river away and make way, so that they fear you.'

Jumbe was happy with the idea of bigness, so he wriggled his tail like a string for girls' jumping games. He smiled a toothless smile. She repeated to him like this:

'Jumbe, we want peas, peas, peas. Tomorrow, early in the morning before cockcrow, come to my house and I will give you pea seeds. Then you get your hoes and go to dig in our garden in the jungle across the river.'

Jumbe flapped his ears and said: 'I will.'

Master Hare's mother was called Min-Hare. She also wanted to plant peas. She had lived with famine for one year and almost lost her throat. The throat that tastes no food grows small-small-small-small and finally contracts like a tin full of vacuum. So Min-Hare called Master Hare, her son, to her, and whispered into his ears like this:

'Now Master Hare, my son, you are the cleverest animal in the whole dark jungle. There is nobody cleverer than you. Perhaps your Daddy was cleverer; but that is another story, for another day. Now, Sonny, we want peas, peas, peas, planted in our field beyond the river. Tomorrow morning I will give you pea seeds to go and plant. Do you hear?'

Master Hare looked unhappy, he sulked. You see, he was a lazy, good-for-nothing boy. After twisting his neck, stepping on one leg, and then the other, and pulling frightful faces, he brightened up a bit. He smiled with his eyes and his ears. Then he went near his mother, jumped on her lap and said:

'Mama, you know how much I keya fo you. Chumoyow, I wiy go chu dig. Have za pea seej yweaji – yoasched.'

'Did I hear you right, Sonny? Did you say the pea seeds should be roasted, really roasted?'

'Zach ywaich,' answered her son, sitting on her lap. 'Yee, Mama, I wanchich yoasched. Zach ich za new meshud.'

'Hm!' wondered Min-Hare. 'Whoever heard

seeds were to be roasted before planting? This, indeed, is a new method.'

'Mama, zach ich za new feshun. Eveyebojy ich doing yaik zach,' answered her son, jumping from her lap and running to eat the remains of the previous night's potatoes in the pot in their kitchen.

Very early in the next morning, Jumbe Elephant took his sack full of pea seeds, and five blacksmith-new hoes with him. Master Hare took his bag of roasted peas, and one hoe. Jumbe Elephant and Little Hare met on the way to their gardens, just outside their separate courtyards. The path was full of grass, which was heavily loaded with big morning dew. Master Hare did not want to walk in the dew, so he jumped up and down and cried as if Satan had come to fetch him to hell. Jumbe was touched with pity. He asked his friend:

'My friend, what is the matter?'

Master Hare fell down on his back and rolled on the ground like an earthworm. He continued to cry. Jumbe asked him again:

'My friend, what is the matter? Are you ill?'

Then Master Hare stopped crying, and, while wiping tears from his eyes with the back of his hands, sobbing, and blowing his nose, answered like this:

'My fiyend, Mascha Eyephanch. You know I am

veye shoch. I cannoch walk in zich yong wech
guyach. Cayyi me on yoya back, peyeach?'

Jumbe Elephant realized that, indeed, his friend
was short, that he could not walk in the long wet
grass, and that it would be better for him to carry
Master Hare on his back. He then said:

'Come on, my friend, I'll carry you,' and lifted
Master Hare who was holding a hoe in one hand,
and the bag of peas in the other, and put him on his
back. He carried Master Hare right to his field,
placed him down, and then went to his own garden
to dig.

Jumbe Elephant dug, and dug, and dug, since
sunup till sundown. He dug a whole valley and a
hill. Altogether he used up five blacksmith-new
hoes.

Master Hare just sat down where Jumbe had
placed him. He opened the bag and tasted one
roasted pea. It was very saliva-bringing. He took
another, and ate it. You see, his mother was a very
good cook and had put the right amount of salt on
the peas. Master Hare's saliva started to flow like a
dog's. He ate all the pea seeds from the top of the
bag right to the bottom. He then held the bag with
the left hand and pushed his right hand to the
bottom. He found scarcely a pea. So he again held
the bag bottom-side up, and hit it so hard that all
broken pieces of peas fell on his upturned hand. He
overturned these into his mouth and ate them.

Now that there were no more peas to eat, he smacked his mouth, and thought of going to the river to drink some water in order to top off his satisfaction. It was already midday, and there was no more dew on the grass. So Master Hare started going home. While crossing the river between his home and the field, he drank some water. After that, he dived inside the water so that he looked like a man wet with sweat. He came home with a full stomach.

When he reached home, Min-Hare, his mother, asked him like this:

'Sonny, how was the digging?'

Master Hare stood up and held his back with his hand like a tired old woman, and then replied:

'Oh! Oh! Oh! Jigging was veye veye haj. I jug tiy my back eked and my bojy eked veye veye mach.'

'Very good, you are doing fine Sonny, you are doing just like your father. I am sure this year we shall have plenty of peas.' So spoke the pleased Min-Hare.

The next day Master Hare took with him a bigger bag of roasted peas. He cried again when he saw his friend Jumbe. Jumbe carried him to the field. Jumbe then went to his own field again to dig. This time he completely dug through two valleys and two hills and used up ten blacksmith-new hoes. Master Hare again ate all his roasted peas and came back with a stomach full as a cook's. During all the planting season Jumbe dug; Master Hare ate.

Now it was time for harvesting peas. Min-Hare called her son, Master Hare, to her and talked to him like this:

'Sonny, your peas should be ready for harvesting now. You had said your new method makes peas grow faster. Tomorrow, go and get us a basketful of peas. I am tired of eating dry meat, smoked meat, roots, and fruits. I want to taste the peas of the season.'

Master Hare frowned, twisted his eyebrows, and looked like a child who is being forced by his mother to swallow quinine. He felt like crying, and turned his head away from his mother. Then he cheered up a little. You see, he had to cut wisdom. He then approached his mother with his small white tail tucked in between the legs, and looked humble and obedient. He rubbed his hairy body against his mother's and told her:

'Jear Mama, waich foy anaja week. I wench chu za gayjen yischajei and founj za pea noch yweji.'

She said to him:

'All right. All right, Sonny. If you say that you went to the garden yesterday and found the peas not ready, I believe you. I will continue to eat the hard food for another week.'

That week passed, rather too quickly for Master Hare.

One day, Min-Hare went to visit Min-Jumbe, Jumbe Elephant's Mother. Min-Jumbe cooked well-fried fresh peas with onions and curry powder, and other Eastern spices. Min-Hare had never eaten such a nice meal before. She ate, and ate, and ate, till she even ate one of her fingers. She then stopped eating and looked like a woman growing two children in her stomach. She thanked Min-Jumbe. Min-Jumbe thanked her dutiful son. Jumbe was so proud that he flapped his ears, jumped about, and smiled, and smiled till his eyes were as small as full stops.

That evening, Min-Hare came home crawling. She was oversatisfied with food and angry with her son. She called him to her and commanded him:

'Sonny, tomorrow you must get us peas from your garden. Your friend's have been ready for cooking long ago. Min-Jumbe is already eating this year's peas. But you still let your own mother eat dry food. Why do you treat me as if I have no son?'

Master Hare twisted his neck left and right, and came to his mother. She pushed him away. He came again but was pushed away. Then he said to his mother like this:

'Mama, Oy-ywaich.'

It was all right. That night, everybody in the

village slept soundly except Master Hare. You see, he had tricked his mother into roasting all the peas; roasted peas cannot grow. Roasted peas are good for eating, and that is exactly what Master Hare had done with the seeds. Now, that night, he stayed awake in his bed turning from side to side. He had to cut wisdom.

Very early in the next morning, Master Hare went quickly through the wet grass to Jumbe's home. He hid behind their house, listening. Presently, he heard Min-Jumbe send her son to the pea garden. She told Jumbe to bring her the fresh peas from the garden quickly because, after cooking the midday meal, she wanted to go to visit her own friend, Min-Hippo.

Jumbe went and returned, carrying on his strong back a load of peas as big as a bus.

When Master Hare saw that Jumbe had returned from the garden, he reasoned like this: today Jumbe will not go to the field again; therefore, I can go and steal from his garden. Master Hare then jumped up and ran like this: tip-tip-tipiti-tipiti-tipiti, and before you could say 'Ha' he had already jumped across the river, and before you could exclaim 'Ho !' he was already in Jumbe's garden.

He harvested like the thief he was: roughly, choosing where the peas looked very good and ripe. He took one or two from here, jumped there and got three and four, and before long, had a sack full of peas. The pea load was so heavy that when he carried it on his head it almost broke his neck; then he tried pulling it on the ground, but feared he would be traced out; then he carried it on his shoulder all the way home to his mother. When he reached there, Min-Hare could not see him. She only saw a large moving sack of peas. She was surprised and afraid. Then she asked:

'What is that?'

A voice from the bottom of the bundle called out:

'Mama, zich ich me – yoya juchifuy chany.'

He then put the peas down and sat under the verandah to rest. His mother came to thank him:

'Sonny, you are the best farmer. Some children don't know how to care for their mothers, but you do. See, you have done better than Jumbe – that friend of yours who is as big as a house but lazier than a satisfied dog.'

Master Hare concurred with her like this:

'Kwaich ywaich, Mama. You nyow when I puch my hach and bojy on chamching I jo za bech.'

And his mother nodded in agreement with her son's praise of himself – that whenever he put his heart and body on something the result was always wonderful.

When Jumbe Elephant went to the field the next morning he was as mad as a man who stepped on fire. He jumped up and down, and his large feet made large holes on the ground from which water began to come. He was mad with rage. He made a loud noise through his long trunk, which brought all animals running: some came trotting, other galloping, birds came flying, snakes came sliding, and insects crawling, and frogs hopped along. The lion came, the leopard came, the hippo, too, the spider was there, so was the cuckoo and the abominable slow man, Mister Snail. They all asked Jumbe this question:

'What is the matter?'

Jumbe answered them like this:

'A thief has stolen my peas.'

And they asked him the next questions:

'Did you catch him? Do you know him?'

'No. I have not caught the bad-doer. I don't know him,' he answered like that, shaking his head.

All the animals of the jungle were very angry. The Good Neighbour Law of the Jungle, as written by Chief Justice Hornbill, reads like this: 'You shall not reap in another's garden without his permission; anybody caught doing so shall be taken to the Court of General Attendance, and, if proved guilty, shall be boiled for all good animals to eat.' That rule made the jungle free of thieves. You see, if you stole once, ate the food, and were found out, you would be eaten too. After that, you would not eat again; dead people don't eat.

So now you know why all the animals were angry, don't you? They thought Jumbe had caught a thief so that they would have free meat to eat on that day!

The following day, Jumbe lay down by his garden waiting to catch the thief. He waited, and waited, thinking every minute: now the thief is coming; now he is almost here; now I shall lift up my head and see him – then he would do so, and see nobody. Actually, Master Hare had gone to steal once more, but he saw Jumbe's big stomach above the grass. Moreover, when food moved in Jumbe's stomach, the rumbling could be heard by a person a half a mile away.

Jumbe waited for a long time. In the evening, when he thought any thief would have despaired and gone home, he went to his mother.

Before his back had completely disappeared from view, his friend, Master Hare, was already inside the field with his big bag on his back. He filled it in no time with peas, and then went home. His mother came to help her heavily laden son when he was near home.

Master Hare was in bed throughout the next day. He had eaten too much of raw peas, half-cooked peas, and cooked peas. His stomach went wrong. So he vomited a potful of peas. His mother put him to bed and covered him to the neck. All the same, he went on vomiting and wetting the bed so that another name for it was stench.

Jumbe went to the garden that morning. He was angry beyond dictionary words. He put his long trunk up and tried to pick the scent of the thief. He could not get it. Then he opened his ears like a big sail, but could hear nothing. He came back to his mother, crying.

Min-Jumbe called him a fool. Why didn't he catch the thief?

So Master Hare went on stealing for one complete month. Jumbe never caught him. Master Hare was getting fat, very fat. But Jumbe was beaten by his mother all the time; he grew thin and resembled the fossil skeleton of an elephant. You know what Min-Elephant did to her son, don't you? She hit him on the back, twisted his tail here and there, pinched his ears, and refused to give him food. She said he must catch the thief.

One evening, Mr Bat came flying blindly, and entered Jumbe's ear. Jumbe took him out, and was about to squash him, when Mr Bat pleaded for mercy.

Mr Bat said, 'Don't kill me.'

Jumbe asked, 'What will you do for me?'

Mr Bat said, 'I will tell you.'

Jumbe asked, 'What?'

Mr Bat replied, 'Ways of catching your pea stealer.'

Then Jumbe brought Mr Bat very near his eyes. Mr Bat told Jumbe his secret:

'In the jungle, if you don't know who stole your things, you take a journey right to Master Knowall, Doctor Witch-Doctor, the Honorable Doctor Tortoise, M.D., D.W.D., etc. She is well-known throughout the whole world for her witchcraft. She knows the answers to questions like: "Why is there only one moon?" "Why people dream?" "Why only women bear children?" "Why we bats can fly but you elephants don't?" "Why big cocks run away when they see a small kite flying?" "Why we have shadows?" and all questions you think of in your heart. I advise you to go to her.'

Jumbe came home and asked his mother to prepare victuals ready for the journey. He took with him roasted groundnuts heavy enough to last a whole month. He was going to find the doctor. On the way, he met Miss Chameleon who asked him why he walked as if he carried the jungle's troubles behind his back. He answered that he was looking for a witch-doctor. Miss Chameleon said she was a competent doctor. She told him to go and lay a trap on the eastern side of the garden. Then she asked for her fees. Jumbe paid much money and went home. He did as he was told. And caught nothing. Meanwhile, Master Hare went on stealing and becoming so fat you would think he would break the weighing scale.

Jumbe had been deceived. Chameleon is no doctor; she deceives as often as she changes the colour of her skin. Jumbe's mother beat him harder and sent him away to find the real doctor. This time he met with the double-mouthed snake, the one which can move as fast in the direction of its tail as it can in that of its mouth, like a reversing train. Master Double-Mouthed, as they called him, also deceived Jumbe.

He came back to his mother. Now he was thinner than the skeleton of an elephant. Mr Bat met him and asked:

'What did Doctor Tortoise say?'

Jumbe looked like a fool, and said he had not yet gone to Doctor Tortoise's. Mr Bat asked why? Jumbe answered that he thought one witch-doctor was as strong as another.

Mr Bat then said, 'Let me tell you, some doctors are better than others; Dr Tortoise is the best of them all.'

The next morning, Jumbe went to Min-Jumbe and asked for more victuals for taking the journey to Dr Tortoise's. He needed to take presents and fees for the doctor. Unfortunately, Jumbe had already wasted the family fortune on false doctors. His mother gave him the little that remained.

When he arrived at Doctor Tortoise's home he found a long line of clients, as long as that of people going to cast their votes. After a long wait, his name was called and he was ushered into the doctor's examination room. The doctor's assistants closed all the windows, and went out, leaving Doctor Tortoise and Jumbe Elephant alone. After the doctor had closed the door behind his assistants, he turned his attention to the client. Jumbe narrated the long history of the clever thief who had been stealing his peas. He emphasized that his only object in life now was to catch the evil-doer.

Doctor Tortoise said he could help Jumbe. But before he could give any help, Jumbe had to pass a certain test. That test was this: whatever he, the doctor, would do, Jumbe had to continuously breathe normally; on no account had he to spit.

Jumbe said he had expected a harder test. He had endured worse things than holding spit. He begged the doctor to go ahead with the test.

Doctor Tortoise then pulled one leg inside his shell, then the other; pulled one hand in, and then the other; and at last withdrew his scaly head inside so that no part of him was visible, except the shell. Then, he broke wind like this:

'Doo-oot,' just like the blowing of a trumpet or a school bugle.

The smell of Doctor Tortoise's gas was like that of a rotten egg mixed with ammonia. It went right through Jumbe's long nose, inside his long stomach, and before he realized it, he had not only spat, but sickened and vomited right on the clean floor of the examination room. Doctor Tortoise quickly reappeared from the shell and ordered his special police to escort Jumbe right off his premises. You see, Jumbe had failed the test.

Jumbe went home again. His mother almost died when she saw her foolish boy. But once a boy is yours, foolish or clever, poor or rich, obedient or disobedient, you will keep him and help him. No elephant ever deserts a son.

Jumbe had to return to Doctor Tortoise again. He had promised his heartbroken mother that this time he would be as brave as a man, and endure everything.

He found Doctor Tortoise was ready. In the examination room the doctor broke the wind and it was quite a stench. Jumbe said I will spit it out. Doctor said don't. Jumbe said it is very pungent. Doctor said please swallow it. Jumbe said it is rotten. Doctor said shut up. Jumbe said I will die. Doctor said be a man. Swallow it. Quick. Then Jumbe closed his eyes tightly and swallowed like this:

'Boo-rooch!'

Doctor Tortoise was glad, and congratulated Jumbe on his passing the test.

Immediately, Jumbe was changed into a new person. He neither hesitated, dodged, procrastinated, nor feared. As soon as he thought of a thing, he went and did it. He also did all the things he was told. Nobody in the beastly jungle was as strong, obedient, and skilful as Jumbe.

Doctor Tortoise then told him what to do. He was to go and rob beehives of beeswax and of the sticky gum. The doctor further gave him this instruction:

'Make a beautiful, very beautiful, girl from the gum of bees. Place that beautiful girl in your garden where the peas are excellent. Leave the figure there, before long, I tell you, you will catch your thief. Good hunting.'

Meanwhile, Master Hare had been fattening on the stolen peas. He took six meals during the day, and three at night. He would now harvest three miles of Jumbe's pea garden at a time. One day, he woke up in his bed, and yawned, and stretched his hands and legs, and spoke to himself like this:

'Chujay, I wiy yeep anj yeep fife yivach of peach.'

He then hurried that day to go and reap five rivers of peas. He reached Jumbe Elephant's pea garden in the cool hour of the evening, and – Lo! Behold! There was a very beautiful girl. A girl with the best combed and oiled hair, the whitest teeth, the best smile, the most elegant neck, the

D

71

cleanest and smoothest body, and the straightest and finest breasts.

'Whew!' whistled Master Hare, in admiration. He pushed his hands into his pockets, muttered to himself that this was the mother of all beauties. He then stared at her, stretched his neck and stood on his hind legs like an animal in a circus, and continued to stand there struck with this beauty. Then he did what you would do when you saw a beautiful girl: he went to her. He came with his hands in his pockets and walked proudly around her, admiring her up from toe to hair, and then down from hair to toe. He shook his loving head and said:

'Zich ich veye beochifuy.'

And, indeed, that was very beautiful.

'Gooch moynying?' he greeted her, smiling. Master Hare was sure that each time he talked to her, she broadened her smiles specially for him. He went nearer her and repeated his greetings:

'Eh, Maja-in-Yaw'ch doucha, gooch moynying? How are you chujay?' He got more smiles and no verbal answers from his mother-in-law's daughter who did not answer his good mornings.

He shook his head and thought: look at this beautiful girl. She is so proud she can't even answer my greetings. Then he went to her and said:

'Eh, Mich Beochifuy, Mich Yunyiverch, jonch be cho pyouj. How manyy beochifuy guych jo yu chink I have nyyony?'

You see, he was angry. The girl could have been Miss Universe, but she should not have been so proud, because, as everybody knew, Master Hare had known many more beautiful girls.

'Mich Beochifuy, how are you?' asked Master Hare, extending his right hand to shake hers. But the hand stuck hard in the sticky beesgum. Master Hare tried to pull his hand out but it would not come. He pulled so hard he almost tore it off at the shoulder.

'Wey,' Master Hare said, 'if you jonch wanchchu speak chu me, yeave my hanj.' But the hand was never freed. So, in anger, he pushed her with his left hand in an attempt to wrench his right one free. But both hands now stuck fast in the girl made of beesgum. Master Hare was very mad. He tried to free himself by scratching on the ground with his hind legs. His legs revolved as fast as those of a bicyclist. He could not become free, however hard he struggled. Then he cried thus in an angry voice:

'Ma-ma, Ma-ma!! Come chu heyp me! I am couch.'

Who should hear his cry for help, but Jumbe Elephant? Jumbe heard the cry when he was taking supper. He left the meat, bread, butter, tea, milk, cassava, potatoes, and yams, and ran. He ran; he was on the rampage. He tore trees down, trampled grass down, stepped on snakes and rats and any living thing on his way. He ran with his tail standing up straight – straight like a yard rule, his ears were opened like umbrellas, and the trunk was up, as if he was possessed by a legion of evil spirits.

Then he blew through his nose loud and clear calling all the birds and animals of the jungle to come to see the thief.

When he came near the thief, whom did he find to his consternation but his bosom friend Master Hare? He hit him hard on the head, and exclaimed:

'What in the Jungle are you doing here?'

All of the animals of the jungle ran to Jumbe's field to see the wrongdoer. The hyena came, the owl too, and the buffalo, the lion, the sheep, and all those animals whose pictures you see in biology books.

Min-Jumbe, Jumbe's mother came. Master Hare's mother, called Min-Hare also came. When Min-Hare saw that it was her son who was trapped, she shrieked and breathed once. That's all. She never breathed again. She fell down – dead.

The animal Court of General Attendance decided, according to old-time custom, that Master Hare, the thief, had to be boiled, and eaten by everybody. Jumbe Elephant who caught the thief was to boil him, to supply the peas, and bread to go with the feast. He was to cook a feast for the seventy thousand animals and birds, and insects of the jungle.

Jumbe Elephant felt sorry for his friend. He had not suspected him of the theft. He did not want to boil or eat him. But Min-Jumbe told him to go ahead with the court ruling; even if he would not eat the boiled Master Hare, he should not defy the court ruling. Even the laws of the Jungle have to be respected. With a heavy heart and much reluctance, Jumbe gathered firewood for boiling his friend, Master Hare. After Master Hare had pleaded in vain for mercy, he resigned himself to his fate. His death rid the jungle of a master thief.

You see, if you do bad things, you may escape discovery once, but one day you will be caught. If you are caught, you will be punished. That is what my story about Master Hare and his friend Jumbe Elephant teaches us.

FIXIONS

'WELL, I have come to talk to you about that project you approached our government about – the one requiring about two million dollars – building a road to your home and a bridge?'

'Yes. Yes. Yes. I was beginning to think you had refused us the grant and I was beginning to search elsewhere.'

'Oh. Be patient. The President, my President, has had a hell of a lot of trouble getting foreign aid approved this year. You know we are tied down in that war of liberation in Vietnam and that is consuming most of our attention and money. But he has been able to just get a little sum of money granted. You were marked down for priority treatment. He himself has sent you this.'

'Oh, thank you very much. Thank you very much. You are really good people.'

'We are friends, *your* friends.'

'Of course. Of course.'

'And our local businessmen. . . .'

'Yes? Your businessmen?'

'And our businessmen here have decided to give

you and your wife, I am sorry, your first lady, gifts.'

'Wonderful. Wonderful. Where are they? Let me see them.'

'Here they are. This gold wristwatch is for you. This pendant watch is for your wife, first wife, I mean. I am sorry again.'

'Oh don't mind. Thank you very much. WIFE? WIFE? MY MOTHER HOUSE? ...'

'Eh, stop hollering. What are you calling her here for? It is too late to wake your wife up – I mean your first lady.'

'She simply has to come and see these. That woman has to see the gift given her by her friends.'

'No, no. Let her sleep. Besides we have not yet finished our major business.'

'Yes. Yes. Let's continue. I had momentarily forgotten. When do you give me the money?'

'Any day. Tomorrow if you wish. Where shall it be banked?'

'My account is with the National Bank.'

'You will get it there tomorrow.'

'Thank you. It should earn me quite a bit of interest.'

'What is that you say?'

'Oh. Nothing much.'

'By the way, what tips have your intelligence men given you?'

'Tips? Tips? What tips?'

'Information, man, about your state and your life.'

'None. As far as I am aware we are peaceful.'

'Oh, yeah? I thought your intelligence chaps were smarter than that.'

'Why?'

'It has been brought to my attention, most reliably, that three days from today you are to be murdered and the leader of the opposition is to become the President. Listen to this very carefully. This chap (you know who I mean, without having names?) has been organizing things. And by the end of the month he and your lieutenant (you know who I mean) intend to stage a successful and swift coup. Tomorrow they are receiving the last consignment of arms and other aids from (you know the place), ('Oh! Oh!'). Yes. And they intend, I hate to repeat it, though to you I must, to have you killed till you are dead. You, your wife, pardon me again, first lady I meant, and your children are all to be wiped out from the face of the earth.'

'This is unbelievable. To think that . . .'

'I didn't believe it at first. But knowing this man and those in whose pay he is, I say, knowing these heartless people, I doubted and doubted till I believed that unbelievable as the intelligence is, it is, nevertheless, true. He has been opposing you. Why? To amuse himself? You are less naïve than that. It was of course to rally a following.'

'Oh my God! My God! To think that I worked hard to help him. And my deputy. To think that I spent my own money to raise him from the streets, get him a seat in parliament, and a cabinet post – impossible, quite impossible.'

'My dear friend, even the great Caesar could not believe his eyes when he saw Brutus strike the first blow.'

'Very bad. Very bad.'

'Yes. But what are you going to do? Mumble: very bad, very bad? You had better act, man, while there's still time. The best defence is an attack. You had better begin. The opposition is not waiting, nor philosophizing as you are. Act! Do something. Why keep troublemakers loose, anyway? The best place for them is the prison or firing squad. I suggest you round these local chaps up and drive away their foreign supporters. . . . How can we give you this aid when you are no longer there?'

'All right then. Thank you very much sir. Thank you for all your aid. We shall take care of these traitors. Thank you again.'

'Oh, don't mention it.'